To read fluently is one of the basic aims of anyone learning English as a foreign language. **And it's never too early to start.** Ladybird Graded Readers are interesting but simple stories designed to encourage children between the ages of 6 and 10 to read with pleasure.

Reading is an excellent way of reinforcing language already acquired, as well as broadening a child's vocabulary. Ladybird Graded Readers use a limited number of grammatical structures and a carefully controlled vocabulary, but where the story demands it, a small number of words outside the basic vocabulary are introduced. In *The Pied Piper of Hamelin* the following words are outside the basic vocabulary for this grade:

everywhere, get rid of, lame, mayor, pipe, rat, tune

Further details of the structures and vocabulary used at each grade can be found in the Ladybird Graded Readers *leaflet.*

A list of books in the series can be found on the back cover.

British Library Cataloguing in Publication Data
Ullstein, Sue
   The Pied Piper of Hamelin.
   I. Title   II. Price Thomas, Brian
   III. Browning, Robert, *1812-1889*. Pied Piper of Hamelin
   428.6'4
   ISBN 0-7214-1211-4

First edition

Published by Ladybird Books Ltd Loughborough Leicestershire UK
Ladybird Books Inc Auburn Maine 04210 USA

© LADYBIRD BOOKS LTD MCMLXXXIX
All rights reserved. No part of this publication may be reproduced, stored in a retrieval system, or transmitted in any form or by any means, electronic, mechanical, photo-copying, recording or otherwise, without the prior consent of the copyright owner.

Printed in England

The Pied Piper of Hamelin

written by Sue Ullstein
illustrated by Brian Price Thomas

Ladybird Books

This is the town of Hamelin.
It is a good town
but…

There are a lot of rats —
big rats and little rats —
rats in the shops
and rats in the houses.
There are rats
everywhere!

The people of Hamelin do not
like the rats. They want
to get rid of the rats.

A man says, "What can we do?
There are rats everywhere!"

The people say, "We'll go to see
the mayor. He'll help us."

The people go to see the mayor.
"Please, please get rid of
the rats," they say.

The mayor says, "I don't like
the rats, but what can I do?
There are rats everywhere!"

"You must get rid of the rats," the people say. "You are the mayor of this town."

They go home.

A man comes to the town.
He has a pipe.
He is the Pied Piper.

The Pied Piper goes to see the mayor.

"I can help you," the Pied Piper says. "Give me some money. I'll get rid of the rats."

"Yes, please help me,"
the mayor says. "If you
get rid of the rats,
I'll give you some money."

The Pied Piper is happy.

The Pied Piper plays a tune on his pipe. All the rats in Hamelin follow the Pied Piper...

Big rats and little rats,
fat rats and thin rats —
they all follow the Pied Piper.

They like his tune.

The Pied Piper comes to a river. He stops but his tune goes on. All the rats jump into the river.

Soon all the rats are dead.

The Pied Piper goes to see the mayor.

"All the rats are dead," the Pied Piper says. "I must go now. Please give me my money."

"No," the mayor says. "I won't give you the money. The rats are dead and you must go. We don't want you in Hamelin."

"Give me my money, please," the Pied Piper says.

He is angry.

"If you don't give me my money, I'll play a different tune!" he says.

"Play a different tune," the mayor says. "But I won't give you the money."

So the Pied Piper plays
a different tune on his pipe.

The children of Hamelin
are playing with their toys.
They hear the Pied Piper's tune.
They like it.

Boys and girls, big children and little children – they all follow the Pied Piper.

The Pied Piper comes to the river, but the children do not jump in. The Pied Piper goes on and the children follow him.

They come to a mountain.
The mountain opens.

The Pied Piper and the children go into the mountain. There is a beautiful garden inside the mountain.
There are trees
and flowers.

Then the mountain closes.
One little boy walks very
slowly. He is lame.
He wants to go into
the mountain, too.
But he cannot go in.

The lame boy goes back to the town. He has not got any friends now. All the children of Hamelin are inside the mountain.

The mayor looks everywhere for the children and the Pied Piper, but he cannot find them.

The people of Hamelin never see their children again.